Walking with Grandpa

by Liz Stenson

Illustrated by Stéphane Jorisch

I love to go walking
with Grandpa.

Grandpa stops to talk
to the neighbours.

So do I.

Grandpa stops to look
at the boats.

So do I.

Grandpa stops to smell
the flowers.

So do I.

Grandpa stops to get a book.

So do I.

Grandpa stops to get money.

So do I.

Grandpa stops to look
at the bikes.

So do I.

I stop to get ice cream.
So does Grandpa!

16